the afterlife is a hangover

poems by
Jason Baldinger

art by
Nell Hendricks

STUBBORN MULE PRESS

copyright 2020 Jason Baldinger (poetry) & Nell Hendricks (art)
cover design: Nell Hendricks
ISBN: 978-1-950380-96-1
LLOC: 2020932505
Stubborn Mule Press
Devil's Elbow, MO
stubbornmulepress.com

*The motel of lost companions waits
with heated pool and bar.*

—Neil Young
Thrasher

For Karl

and all my friends who've stared down the barrel,
no matter whether they've won or lost.

Fuck Cancer

I

the road back from Connecticut
            racing

                        racing

don't know why
no reason to hurry
I'm underemployed
boohoo most of America is

ninety miles an hour through New York
one hundred across Interstate Eighty
log jammed on Ninety-Nine pedal down
all in on the Sheetz Highway

it was good to be with family
the last six weeks were silence
winter cocoons   barely working

two days in a record store
one day tossing drywall
twenty-five hours
three hundred a week
to cover life and living
money runs quick
even on grilled cheese
or peanut butter and jelly
washed with box wine

I remember a laundromat conversation
with a plumber the *key* to making
an unorthodox schedule work

all the work I can handle
a hundred a day
cash under the table
more if he was paid more

I should be high on the hog
after that first Morningside arctic day
I didn't hear from him

I call   voicemail
I call   nothing this week

end of February
the drywall guy
pries out the truth
cancer   liver cancer
not much time to live
plumber's wife says
all he does is sit in a chair
smokes Kools   stares at TV

tonight, I race
not giving a shit about the ticket
or how to pay for it

cancer
is just a word
a dim bulb
in the back of my mind

the only thing I can think
this path is untenable

things need to change

Jason Molina
on the stereo
sings
the real truth about it is
is no one ever gets it right
the real truth about it is
we all have to try

racing tonight
racing decisions
racing mind
knowing home will be worse
not sure where the fuck else to go

II

I'm short on work again this week
Richard calls
he runs Surplus Anxiety Records
he took over from Pete
who had it twenty years

Richard was here before Pete
twenty-three years
it was called Jack's when he started
Richard has worked here since he was a kid
that's why he bought it
it's the truth when he says

he didn't know what else to do

Richard struggles
phone chokes
voice wavers
he says cancer

  cancer

I'm floored
not sure what to say
I mean exactly what
are you supposed to say
there's a script
script ain't enough

he'll know next week
can I work more?
I say *yes   yes*
whatever you need

III

what do you say
when someone tells you
they may be dying?

thin voice
near breaking
eyes full of water

boots full of snow
dripping
    water

    water
sustains life

    water
falls to the floor

so much wasted time
heart beats slow fade

what do you say?

what do you say?

IV

Richard says maybe we close the store
              maybe we start clearance
he doesn't want to be too sick
to deal with the situation
maybe he's already too sick

I ask about prognosis, recovery
he says *surgery*
then radiation
after healing
best case scenario

a few months
worst
his life

if it's a few months
why don't I take over
I'll handle it
it'll be ready
when you're ready

would you really be willing?

I've thought hard about this
practically on fire
no one should lose their livelihood
because they're sick
no one should be forced out

this is the richest country in the world
no human
should lose everything
because of cancer

I say
I'm happy to help
whatever you choose
whatever you need
we can see how it goes
if we have to close, we can
if you beat it it's here for you
either way let's give it a try
either way it's up to you

V

Michelle, Richard's wife
they met twenty three years ago
over the counter at the Jack's

blue hour calls
barely together
she explodes
as storm clouds

voice in shreds
you can tell
she's been crying all day
she hasn't slept

rapid fire ramble
this is one of the worst cancers
most aggressive, mouth cancer
he's got two years
what am I going to do?
what am I going to do?

I don't know
I've been honing vocabulary
I'm still looking
for new words
for sympathy
for comfort

she was nurse
how does one

console former nurses

I tell her
there're so many things
we don't know yet
I'm not saying it's fine
but we're going to figure out
a way to get through this

VI

his cheek
bigger every day
there's a specific
flat hospital smell
a smell of cells
in rebellion
a smell
sans antiseptic

surgery is coming
I've been working with him
learning a job I know
ready for transition

I run the store
I'm the face
    the arbiter of information

I do my best

not to ruin
someone's day
waiting here
with bad news
bombs in my pocket

it's record store day
heavy traffic
lines out the door
I'm medicating
with tequila and donuts

after Pete's closed
Richard and I
sat on the back porch
at The Corner Bar
talked Surplus Anxiety
he was sorry
he didn't have more
but a part time job
was waiting for me
after I took
a couple months
on the road

we raised bottles
cheers
to health and future
here's to success
and twenty more years

VII

eleven hours on an operating table
eleven hours like Christ
      arms outstretched
        feet together
eleven hours to remove
  a tumor from a cheek
eleven hours to take
  a patch of skin from an arm
eleven hours to make
  a new cheek
eleven hours
    how many lymph nodes removed
        from the neck
        from the skull
        from the armpit

eleven hours total
  one wonders
 how much of a man
  can you take
before there isn't any man
     left

VIII

I've worked with Runaway Ron for years
now we don't work together
as he works the days I don't

he stops to see how things are
surgery went as well as expected
the skin graft was rejected
I haven't seen him, I've heard
of gaps in his face
of pus, of disfigurement
no one knows right now
if he's gonna make it

I've had this conversation a lot
Richard's been a fixture
here for two decades
he's curated a store
with great taste
and little eye contact

he's been a fixture
in the local music
scene even longer
thundering across
distortion pedals

Richard is private
as the story got out
friends, customers
people all want to know
how he is
how is recovery

now that I run the store
I'm the arbiter of information
puzzle through feelings, grief

I have to balance
what I can, should tell
about how Richard is doing

I have to show compassion
when exhausted
to people who
ask too much
to people who
don't know
how to process
what you've said

I watch faces tighten
they wrestle language
dig for appropriate words
I watch people walk
away frustrated
no means to help

Ron doesn't know what to do
being powerless
affects us all
differently

he does laps
around the store
paces in circles

I see the disconnect
he's short circuited
to comfort himself

he touches everything in the store

I understand
bad news
rattles us from reality
we reach for anything
to assure us
we're actually here

IX

Michelle does bookkeeping
I drop by Sundays, Wednesdays
she signs the checks
keep everything current
I make sure she's alright

on the porch
she smokes
rain starts
she pours my first dirty martini
we unwind memories

she met Richard in the store in 91
she has the coordinates saved
a screen shot on her phone
a Pavement lp
and The Cure's *Kiss Me Kiss Me Kiss Me*
got her a date
and twenty-one years together

I started shopping at Pete's in '94
fresh outta high school
remember buying a Mad Season lp
from the bargain bin, Richard wrote the sale
he rolled his eyes at me
those days of indie cred long gone

I say
one of my favorite shows ever
was Richard and the original trio
at Luciano's one sweltering night in '95 the
Gesture of Kindness release show
100 people butts to nuts
100 degrees, Richard stalked the stage fields
of distortion pedals bled

she laughs hard
recalls awkward first dates
he barely made eye contact
one night he asked her to come see him play
she was mesmerized
this awkward man suddenly possessed
turns a room, all eyes on him

the rain louder, fierce storm tonight
third martini, both of us
clouded eulogies
both of us near decades
still hoping
we' re too young
to talk about cancer

tonight we're lost in memories
the water of life drains away

                              X

Collins and I
happy hour
liquid dinner
and a working plan

is there a way
to form a business plan
to buy Surplus Anxiety
if it comes to that

we talk about Richard
even with Michelle's insurance
bills are steep

who needs a never endless fear
of losing everything
when you're in danger
of losing everything

Big Arthur approached me
about a benefit show
he and Solomon are launching
a kickstart to ease
lost wages and bills

Collins plans
a literary benefit
Richard exists in both worlds
music and writing
maybe a book of poems
music and Pittsburgh
dedicated to Richard

we are a community
we stand for each other
the way poor people do
anything to ease the need

XI

I spent summer
stopping a few times a week
talk business, numbers, orders

he spends his time in pajamas
in a chair by the television
sick room smell
better than a hospital

I take a deep breath
when I come in
when I leave

I saw him on the street
with Michelle walking home

I saw the way his cheek
was scarred, recessed

shocked
I excuse myself
he notices me staring
even though I'm not

we talk often about his return
he's afraid of emotions
the rush when he crosses the threshold

it's September
autumn sun slips out
I didn't know he was coming
all of sudden here
a ghost in the doorway

XII

we are gathered
we are gathering
more than just a rock show
more than just art show
more than just a reading

we turned Brillo upside down
bands and friends
Richard was too overwhelmed
he had to leave

sometimes it's hard to see
all the hands that hold you

we ballyhooed at Modern Formations
Good Noise in fashion

this city
blue collar as fuck
we celebrate
like we work
harder than hell
before the lid blew off

you never know
if the next day
will come

it's an uneasy alliance
    a mania
but how the hell
can we not celebrate
our lives as friends?

we turned
all the way up
at Roboto
when distortion pedals
drowned our fears

in this town we celebrate life
like it's our fucking job
when they cut the lights

we all fall down

XIII

we spent fall working together
me in the front with customers
him sequestered on a computer
the ghost in the back

occasionally customers ask
I send them back
they talk and wish well
occasionally they get *nebby*
a yinzer term for being all
up in someone's business

Richard's face and bald bits
flash bright red
when they ask too much

we don't talk much
I make suggestions
he shoots them down

when he hears me doing something
not the way he would
he storms up, corrects then argues

I try patience
I know what I'm doing

he's sick
he needs to keep something under control
it's not the easiest situation
it's the situation we have

XIV

Michelle calls them jazz cigarettes
a term that came from a conversation
we were talking slang, shit old men say
I don't remember who used the term first

before Thanksgiving
she calls
the pain is bad
painkillers too harsh
a friend gave them weed
would I come over
with rolling papers

I'll feed you dinner
can you teach him
how to roll a joint?

I'm working with his daughter
she sees the odd look
I tell her about the conversation
we giggle

it's absurd this is illegal

it's pain relief
without harsh side affects
without addiction

we eat dinner
wait till his daughter
heads upstairs

I grab a sheet of paper
no grinder, break buds
tiny pieces
easy for burning
piles of green
a pinch in the paper
        then another

Richard watches intent
Manuel Gottsching playing
papers filled between fingers
lick glue
fold over with indexes
twist then roll

some people smooth it out
so it doesn't look like a twig
with warts, I dovetail
a place for my lip
        for the roach clip

I pull strays bits
from either end
he nods, says

that's very organic

he says, *can you roll another?*
heads to the porch
to spark a newfound oblivion
I roll another

finished,
Richard hasn't returned
I find him, back porch burned
up papers
no smoke

I take a fresh joint
light the end
when it flames
I blow it out
hit it
he hits it

I wind my joints tight
sometimes you gotta untwist
it, to get a good hit I show
him, he nods
his eyes have a different spark
he says again, *very organic*

I roll another
he rolls another
each time he says
very organic

space rock shakes our brains
his hands shake joints thin
he thinks he's got it

in the living room
plaster to the ceiling
we watch strings
from ghost guitars
vibrate

this is the first time
I've ever seen Richard
relaxed

XV

between Christmas and New Years
he's back a few months
the ghost in the back

he tells me
he's feeling better
can I work through January
then go to part time

I'm relieved
this is what you want
what you hope for
victory over cancer

I say *yes*
no problem
we'll work it out
but yes

XVI

the doctor's visit
isn't what's expected
you can't say blindsided
cancer is aggressive
cancer comes back

we sit behind the counter
Richard on the stool in tears
Ron and I hands on his shoulders

water of life drips off boots

water of life drips from eyes

water of life drains away

XVII

it's the same conversation
communication is important
when it comes to cancer

everything is theoretical
everything changes

maybe we close the store
           maybe we start clearance
he doesn't want to be too sick
to deal with the situation
maybe he's already too sick

all I need are a few days
off, I'm happy to keep
this arrangement
but I gotta clear my head

he agrees
we are still awkward
       still fumbling

it's clear to me a year in
I don't have the right words
maybe there are none

our vocabulary for sympathy
leaves us cold in these moments
no comfort, mortal, lonely

XVIII

time moves more slowly
everything's the same
nothing really changes
it's the next step
then the next step

even when the cancer isn't yours
it's hard to maintain autonomy

I answer questions everyday
somedays I'm more sensitive
somedays I grit my teeth and spit
somedays I got nothing

I watch their eyes
try and temper what
I'm saying,
I feel terrible
no matter what I'm saying

basically
we're all
treading water

Jason Molina
on the stereo sings
the real truth about it is
no one ever gets it right
the real truth about it is
we all have to try

XIX

I'll go anywhere
to get away
try to get a hold of myelf
I can't get far
but on alternating weeks
when I have two days off
it's Akron for a reading
or Cleveland for a reading
or Baltimore for a ball game
or Harrisburg just to see how fucking bad
   Harrisburg can be

camping in State College
adopting the old guys conversation
       and campfire next to my tent
they tell tall tales deep
into the night, I smoke
a joint lost in the fire

I wake to morning mosquitos
shoo them away, I inventory
last night's dreams
dreams of life without death
dreams of the words *cancer free*

XX

Good News!
Michelle says
the MRI is negative
the cancer hasn't spread
not in the nervous system
not anywhere

there is a shadow
on the scan
even in remission
cancer leaves its mark

XXI

September comes
he's feeling better
I got a vacation in
I'm feeling better
the store isn't feeling better

he takes me aside
says *its time, I'm sorry*
I have to lay you off
I could still use
a couple days
I might need you more
I have scans
appointments

but I'm sorry
I appreciate all you've done
I have to let you go

XXII

I spent October
taking all the work I could
turns out the drywall guy
tore his rotator cuff
he's out of commission
there's no unemployment check
I'm broke

I got a sweet lp collection
from a local book seller
it nets fast cash
I work for him a day a week
in a warehouse shuffling books

then there's the record store
Richard calls some mornings
asking me to come in
usually I can

it's just enough work
to keep me afloat

all the time off is good
but there is no relaxing

I start clear my mind
another phone call
another scan
maybe cancer of the eye
maybe cancer in the same place again

this disease
isn't meant
to give anyone peace

XXIII

deep in
book warehouse stacks
phone goes off
Richard's sick
wants me to come
close the store
I can't
this pays more
this is frequent
he's not too sick
but he is too sick

I tell him I can be there at five
he says he'll try and stay
there are no guarantees

XXIV

how many times
can one person
be diagnosed
before they reach
the end
of a rainbow?

the real truth about it is
it's not an exact science
the real truth about it is
we're all only guessing

XXV

I have a rule
not the best for my health
if there's a parking spot
in front of Brillo
on the way home
I stop have a night cap

it's a testament
I love this bar
know the bartenders
      the patrons
it's impossible to be anonymous

tonight

the energy is off
I catch Michelle's eye
as I break open the door
Lou gives half of his lungs   sigh

immediately
she's in my arms
not weeping
bawling

what is she going to do?
what is she going to do?
how can she live without him?
how can she watch this, goddamnit?

I can't look her in the eye
if I do, its gonna come
there is a storm behind my eyes
it's been waiting to break for some time
my heart doesn't even beat

I remind her
she has everything to live for
two beautiful daughters
two independent women
that say worlds about her
together, three women
can make more sense
out of the universe
than almost anyone else

this is life and death

death is an afterthought
the afterlife is a hangover

the bar's empty now
she's cried herself out
I'm shaking to keep it together
careful not to let it show

XXVI

between appointments
he tells me someone
made an offer on the store
it may be time to sell
he doesn't want to be too sick
he's already too sick
I say alright

this uncertainty
is too much
I'm here full time
status changes daily

there are no plans
that can hold a candle
in a bucket of water
when our lives are on the line

XXVII

Newman asked
if he was planning a living wake
I laughed, we know how uptight Richard is
it's too hard to let go
I guess it would be for me too
this is the only life we know
no matter what deep state hypnosis may say

I do my best to celebrate
every fucking day
it's all so damn thin
you don't know where the coil ends

we leave our bodies
for a new universe
for a new plain of reality

the universe
is expanding
as it expands
it holds a knife
to our throats

XVIII

she tells me
he's in pain
and out of pot

I text
meeting my guy tonight
would you like me to pick up

she palms
three twenties
gives me a hug

I spend the evening
with Glen Ford westerns
the alchemy
rolling an $1/8^{th}$
to joints

when I'm done
I have one for each apostle
and a skinny j
for jesus

XXIX

some nights it's 1995
some nights time means shit
in the living room
Richard in pajamas
with the original trio
Larry and Tony
waiting on big Arthur

I want to be a geek

wishing it was Luciano's
20 years ago
distortion pedals and sweat
not now when we try
not to acknowledge truth
Tony wants to smoke
Richard grabs one of my joints
Larry cuts up about vodka chasers
how carpet cleaner will fuck you up

Richard's having trouble
with his bong
in that he can't use it
we give pointers
screens and how to pack
we don't have a lighter
wooden kitchen matches
held to the bowl
bubble up
hold it
then
exhale

XXX

I met the prospective owner
he's only willing
to buy the store
if I'm willing to stay

I say yeah
I mean I'm fucking tired
I can't deny that
but like Richard
after twenty years
as a customer
and ten years
working
this place
is as close
to home
as anything
to me

XXXI

we talked business
among the ghosts
of patent leather shoes
we talked history
it's true, the Meat Puppets
once tried to buy acid here
I swear when the sound goes down
I hear forty years rush by
one loud constant song

Blitzkrieg Bop or *She's Lost Control*
TV Party or the *John Coltrane Stereo Blues*
Daydream Nation or *Pretty Persuasion*
Game of Pricks or *Yeah, It's Beautiful Here Too*

The Sonic Rendezvous Band *City Slang*
something obscure by Dylan

yesterday Richard called
for the morning report
he told me he's changed his mind
the third time this week
we're open again, no clearance

we hang by a thread
until the next scan
the last one predicted
he'd measure his life in months

denial clear in nervous speech
can you blame him
if this life is all we have
why the fuck would you let it go?

Matt and I are bullshiting
we started on Ween
who fucking sits through a four-hour show?

it shifts to Mingus
I'll talk Mingus for hours
there's a story in every groove
of *Black Saint and the Sinner Lady*
don't get me started on *Better Git Hit in Your Soul*

Matt worked here nine years
he relates the time
he slept in the doorway

his friends dropped him off drunk, 7am
Richard got in a few hours later
said *Nice life you got there*

I was Matt's replacement
now he runs his own store
he tells me
he was high school high
and showed up for work
waited on one customer
then panicked
ran to back
sat in the dark
alone for hours

Pete, the old owner
loved that story
he'd laugh and tell it all the time

back to business
we talk about future
the gravity in now
but scratch that

let's just fuck off
let's talk all the bands
that ex-employees
played in over the years
there's no beer in the fridge
still I'd cheer's them all

Eddie and the Otters

Boogaloo Gestapo
The Congo Eels
Amoeba Knievel
Sweaty Tools
The Skirt Tasters
The Four Roses
House of Assassins
Sludgehammer
Thee Speaking Canaries
Hurl
Centipede E'est
The Trio
The Rock Band

all of us
we're idiots
passing through

XXXII

Richard calls
we're closing

Richard calls
get ready to start
the clearance sale

Richard calls
the store sale is on
be ready to talk to Jimmy

Richard calls
get ready to start
the clearance sale

Richard calls
the store sale
is back on
Jimmy will be in later

Richard calls
we're closing
get ready for a clearance sale

Richard calls
apologizes
I know this is hard
the store sale is on
Jimmy will be in
to talk about
how he wants to run
the takeover

Richard calls
I don't hear what he says
when the line goes dead
I throw the phone
across the store
and scream

XXXIII

I'm getting used to ruining people's day
I piss off and antagonize
telemarketers on purpose
I need someone anonymous
to take a shit on

it's been confirmed
there's only borrowed time
plans see saw

I can't hide my own face
my own pain
I've got a tenuous grip
I'm ducking constantly

I walk in Brillo
Lou looks, says
brother, I think you need a shot

I nod
defeated
down the shot
we exchange a hug

I called Silsbe earlier
he's coming to meet me
I've gotta drop the bomb
I don't want to

he walks in

Lou stands
across the bar
from me

Silsbe says *what's up?*
Lou give him a shot
he's now a colorless Silsbe
Lou says, *you're gonna want that shot*

XXXIV

Pale Blue Eyes on the juke
it's haunting me lately

Lou asks how it is
over the last few years
he's become bartender confidant
we talk cancer and business
over the chemical smell
of a freshly wiped bar

tomorrow is the announcement
I'm not sure
is this the culmination
or a beginning
my relationship with time
has become strange
perhaps more fluid
as I watch the grace of going

it's odd to as we've come closer
to some actual plan
just how fast the world moves
    how we let things go
without a thought
when Richard stops in the store
I wonder what he feels
but I can't ask
our emotions tied so closely
by all these years of Surplus Anxiety

then comes the sale
the papers will say for health reasons
the questions will be invasive
still you can't just say someone is dying

I lie
Richard has outlived
his prediction
this is the bonus round

this disease strips you of everything
I suppose the world does too
it moves on as if nothing happened
if I were wiser, or thinking universally
I may agree with that
what happens here is nothing
a blip on the radar of time
that doesn't change anything tonight
I cheers Lou on buying the bar
his wife and I laugh over
Liquor Control Board hearing questions

we talk about what's changing
something about a sixteen-foot shark
something about a zeppelin
life goes on
I suppose

XXXV

Better Luck Next Year
should be tattooed
on the backs of all our eyes

Ally is thirty-nine
she's been going through
various stages of
superhero training
for two years

her new book
tells the story
recovery
survival
breast cancer is a motherfucker
any cancer is a motherfucker

she reads poems
the air goes out of the room
I stand in the back
lean on bookshelves
brace myself

when I hear her words
I can't keep from crying

the real truth about it is
we're not meant to be warriors
the real truth about it is
there is only unfairness to this life

XXXVI

it's a few days before the last day
I can't count all my last days
over the last nine years

I stop, camel up
on Indian buffet
every Friday
before heading
to the store

Richard and Michelle
are eating, I join them

I want to ask him
how he feels
how it feels
to let go
of the thing
the one thing
be it anchor

or albatross
that holds us in place

it's an oversimplification
there's more to life than one thing
but this disease
strips it all away
leaves one word
on your tongue
survival

XXXVII

when the store changed
ownership five years ago
we downed tequila
and donuts for breakfast

we drank in the nasty alcoholic bar
we all avoided for years
it was a punchline
I can't take anymore
I'm going to Pollock's

it's still a punchline

I remember clinking
glasses that night at
The Corner Bar
toasting to twenty years

that thought sticks
in my throat all day

Richard and family
come later
his girls grew up
here in this store
with the torch passing
a piece of their childhood slips away

the new owner is changing things
he wants to get younger, hipper
shit, I'm forty, he's almost sixty
there is no hipper
I don't even know if I want to stay
but I can't give this up yet
I need to work my way out

when Richard bought the store
five years ago, we came in the day after
inventoried stock to consummate the deal
I remember that awkward moment
five of us standing around
the thanks for everything moment
that last day on earth feeling
I had to leave
my eyes filling
when I walked out
even though I was coming back
it still felt like something slipped away

I head to Brillo

cut cake, remember
drink to Richard's health

we talk deeply for a second
I tell him, I don't know
I'm not sure if I want to do this
without you, it seems strange
he nods we're both a little stuck
our eyes too embarrassed, honest
for our brains, our mouths
to know what we should say

XXXVIII

walking past the tea house
Penn Avenue in August
Garfield wakes to gentrification
I see Jack through the open windows
wave, he knows me as a customer
we cheated at bar trivia together one night

I've got cats to feed, I don't stop
on the sidewalk he calls my name
asks about the store change
lukewarm
but I've got a blank check to restock

he asks how Richard is
on my guard momentarily
then I realize Jack has been though this

he was given a short time to live
he's still here

it's difficult to think about the moment
when someone tells you
you can measure a life in months
in Richard's case, three months
Jack and I agree
this is the bonus round
time exists as a premium
it can always end

I think no matter how much
cancer sucks
it puts time in perspective

I still find language inadequate
when it comes to sympathy
I believe we form relationships
to further language
with the people we love
our best friends
definitely with our lovers
we have a special language
invented in groups and twos
words or phrases
built on experience

like Richard
I'm learning to let go
I'm still am not sure how to explain
or even how to perfect it

I've become blunt
about my own depression
the struggles with our own brains
when our brains are our enemy

we have an image of ourselves in time
we think we have a notion of the future
we think in terms of goals
put premiums on time
none of that really fucking matters

all that matters
Jack and I
maybe Richard
too would agree
is what you do with now

XXXIX

Michelle texts
her mother died
would I have a drink with her
and Kate at the Tikki bar?

I text back
Kate is late
I head to Michelle's
her, Richard and I

talk about her mother's death
her last words
don't be afraid Michelle

I can't fathom
how you talk to your spouse
about you mother's death
when your husband
is reduced to apologies
sorry for cancer
sorry for dying

I talk about my grandmother's death
a month in and out of consciousness
after a stroke took most of her spark
my brother and I spent August nights
hospital picnic benches, smoked
talked our goodbyes for her to each other

she died mid afternoon
I was late
caught in a storm
believe it or not
timed to the moment
she passed

they waited till I was there
they pulled the sheet
sometimes you have plenty
of time to say goodbye
sometimes you have none

in this bar
time fades
we get to stories
Kate ribald
Michelle dry
I keep it silly
but can't stop staring
at Michelle's finger
her dead mothers ring

the third zombie
unties her tongue
leaves a wide-eyed bartender
and nets us a discount

these nights, adrift on time expired
I think in prayers
bless the women who smoke
bless the women who say fuck
               graceful, gossamer, vulgar
bless the way we break to pieces
bless us when pretend to keep it together
and bless the bartenders who delivers drinks
       that for a moment   keeps the pain away

XL

Richard sells records
he bought to sell online
but he's too sick to sell

to work, his life's
his music, his store
have all gotten away

he's started radiation
again
you see him
each time
he comes in
diminishing

I feel awkward
the store isn't the same
it doesn't feel the same to him
when you're dying
how can you worry
about your legacy
when the time left
can be measured
maybe in minutes

XLI

Michelle texts: *Champagne?*
I respond   *would*
she answers in symbols
firecrackers and bottles

I get to Brillo
she pours me a flute

Happy New Year
we both grimace

my unemployment
Richards's new tumors
            nodes of interest
happy anything is bullshit

I change my toast
to the best year possible
our glasses clink

we talk about the beach
we talk about unemployment
we talk about death
she asks, as she does every time
what am I going to do?

over the last months
she's had all kinds of crazy ideas
buying the record store back
opening a bed and breakfast
a recording studio
weightlifting, novelist

after twenty-three years together
and just short of fifty
it must be strange to have a new life
presented from the old
            from the ashes of cancer

I tell her the same thing

keep doing what you're doing
you've managed three years of this
it's not getting any easier
but she's held up better than any of us
she thinks I'm bluffing

we finish the bottle
she doesn't want to go home
but she wants to sit with Richard
watch the ball drop
one last time
unless he's too sick
or the morphine's
already put him to bed

outside, she lights a cigarette
we talk a few minutes
listless in the cold
she drops her cigarette
I give her a hug, say again
here's to the best year possible

XLII

I arrive at Silsbe's
eating a cookie
half full of dope

Michelle calls

they need a witness
for the advanced medical directive
could I stop over and sign

I'm not completely sure what that is
vocabulary words
meant to take the sting out
of what we really mean

I show up in minutes
buzz coming on strong
Richard and I
were gonna hang out tonight
watch hockey with our friends
it's clear
it's too late for hanging out

at the dining room table
he can't make eye contact
when he does he quickly pulls away

I ask him how he's feeling
he says, *scared*
I'm not sure it's the first time
it's the first time our eyes agree

I try small talk
but I'm welcomed
not welcome
this is the start of a vigil
unless the vigil
starts at diagnosis

I gather myself
happy to be too stoned
to admit I'm frightened

I know he won't take a hug
I know if I gave one neither of us
would hold what we have inside

instead, I hold his shoulder
offer him good night
I hope to see you soon

XLIII

over drinks Michelle says
he said something
about dying
she went to answer him
at this moment
in the sentence
she should burst
into tears
instead
a deep breath
an ellipsis in the sentence

she says
you know
ultimately
it's just a natural part of life

XLIV

I'm hanging a porch ceiling
Tuesday afternoon
when she calls, says
hospice

...

hospice
starts this week
maybe
two weeks left
maybe

I acknowledge
I heard
affirmative
ask how she is
nothing lands

ten minutes later
I've fractured
all the calls
    the plans
I can't slow down
my mind

you never feel the punch
till long after it lands

XLV

we were up late
long after everyone
had gone to sleep
Jay and Ally and I
in that farmhouse in Orrtanna
we gotta get up
for the march in DC
in five hours
but we started talking feminism
the conversation got bold
the conversation got deep
we've opened scars
to challenge our thinking

I smoke a joint on the porch
fog so thick
I've faded
reduced
to one cherry
in a white sea

on the divan
can't get comfortable
brain on fire
weed won't slow it down
sofa too small
I don't see the phone light

I get up after an hour
smoke the rest of the joint

back in the farmhouse in Orrtanna
the phone lights again
I know and I don't know
what's waiting for me

his youngest daughter
voice shocked
pleading
full of deference
it sounds like one of his songs

you should come here now
if you want
my mom needs you
or would like
or I would like
where are you?
my dad died tonight

all I say over and over
shit shit shit shit shit

I muster I'm in Orrtanna
I haven't slept
the fog is dangerous
I'll be there in the morning
I'll be there soon as I can

hang up

...
silence
...

there is no one to wake up

alone
on a divan
in a farmhouse in Orrtanna

I won't sleep tonight
I'll sit here
death on my chest
too familiar darkness

I hear stirring upstairs
wait on first light
for goodbyes
as friends come to the living room
of a farmhouse in Orrtanna
I'm try to find an artful way
to tell them
our friend
has died

Jay and Ally
Kris and Anna
they see my
blue hour face
wearing all night
they know
without a word
they know
our friend
has died

XLVI

he was up
he was talking
he was reading
latest issue of Mojo Magazine
he just listened to
the greatest human prayer
A Love Supreme
he asked for a glass of water
Nell got it
went for the porch

they heard a crash
water glass spilled
the struggle started
the struggle never lasts long

the
water
of
life
drained
away

XLVII

Michelle is at the funeral home
making arrangements
for cremation

Big Dan Arthur is upstairs
cleaning the bathroom
running the vacuum

I call hospice for
the bed and oxygen machine
then do the dishes

the house has been full all day
people come and go
the phone rings
the emails pour in
news travels fast

we are all busy
or try to be busy
if only because death
makes us remember
we are all alone

XLVIII

she thinks viewings are garish
he was never religious
why go through that bullshit
I agree

Big Arthur set up a
wake at Brillo
I get there

I ask her how she is
she says, *numb*
she doesn't know where she is
she doesn't think she can do this

she has Atavan
in her purse, I say
today is deep breathes and Atavan
she smiles, says
that that should be a title
to his unwritten last song

XLIX

it's informal
but even informality
needs order
I make things orderly

you never know how
to tribute a friend that's gone
you never know what you'll say

I never thought
I'd mc a funeral
or a wake, whatever

we played his favorite movie
Spinal Tap
both floors filled with friends

who listened, his favorite music
played, a few people wanted
to talk, I introduced them

it took me week of practice
to read his short story
but I did after
we played Neil Young's *Thrasher*
at the mic
I read his story
Stan Getz isn't Coming Back

It ends
don't die
please don't go
you're needed here

as I read it
my voice doesn't crack
        doesn't waiver

the sound goes out of the room
our collective grief
collapsed

I walk off stage
thinking of the the last lines
of *thrasher*

the motel of lost companions
waits with heated pool and bar

sometimes it's hard to see
all the hands that hold you

L

he said
there's a special place
in heaven for me
for all I've done

I appreciate the compliment
but it's unnecessary
we do what we can for people
when we see people need it

that should be the sum
of being human
pay it forward
love each other
best you can

heaven isn't something
I believe in
a bastion for scoundrels
too afraid
to face the life
they've lived

it's this life

the one we are living
that's our reward

Jason Molina
on the stereo tonight sings
the real truth about it is
is no one ever gets it right
the real truth about it is
we all have to try

*Let us cross over the river,
and rest under the shade of the trees.*

—Thomas "Stonewall" Jackson

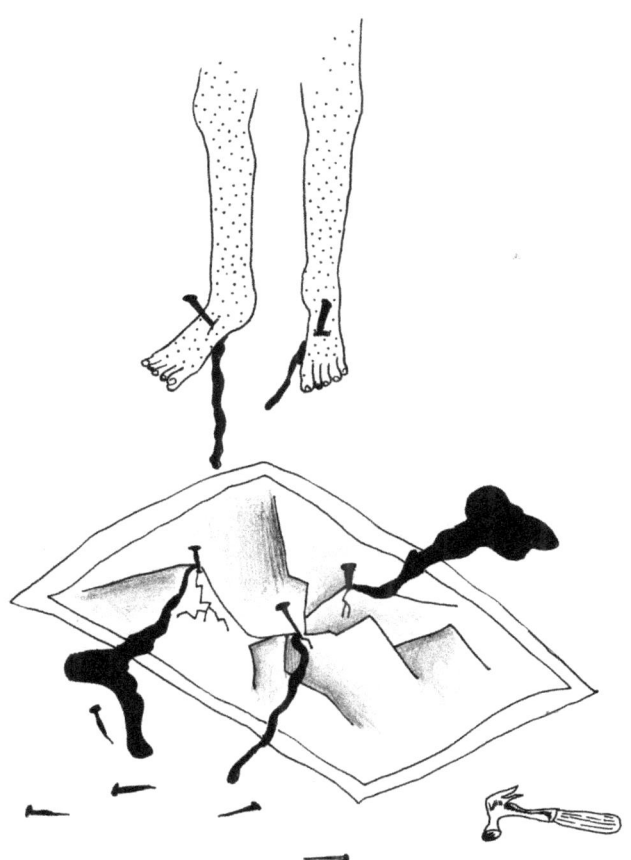

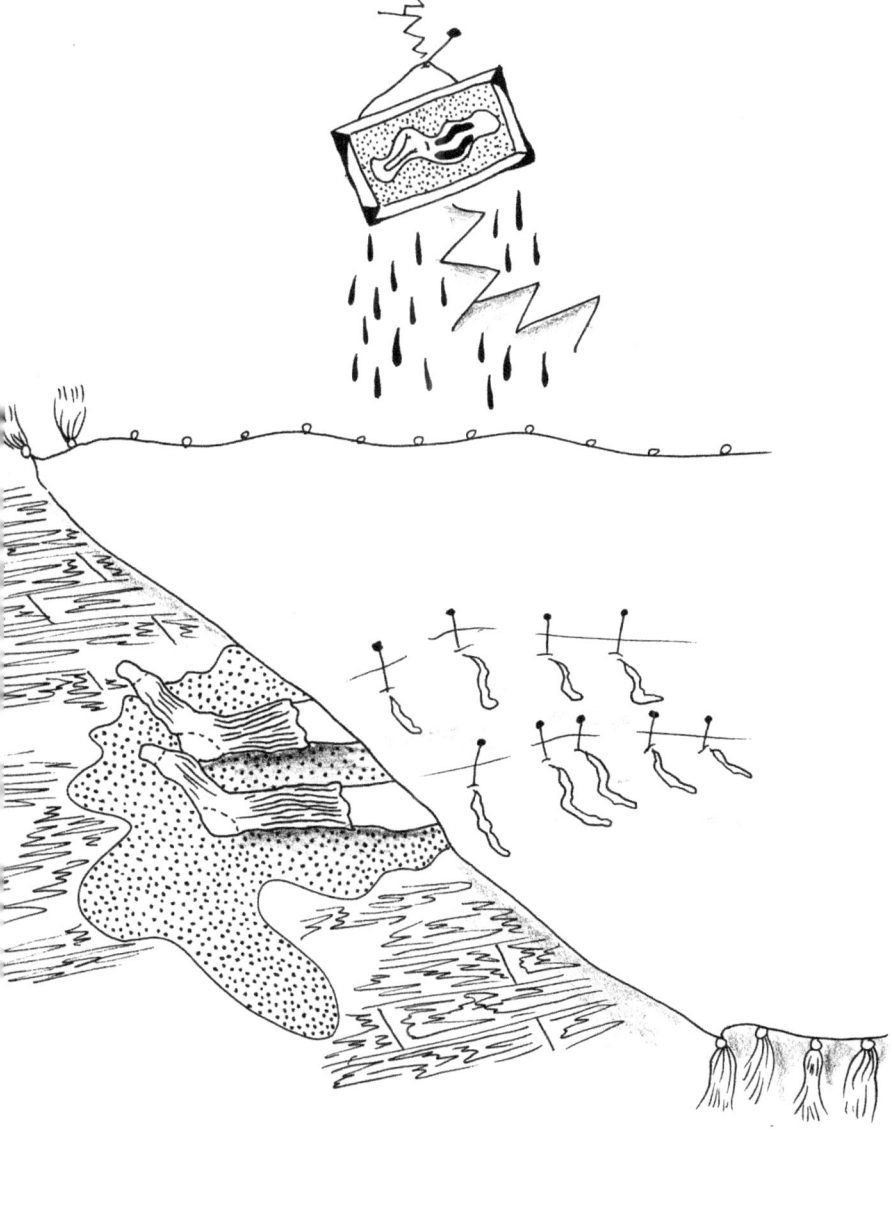

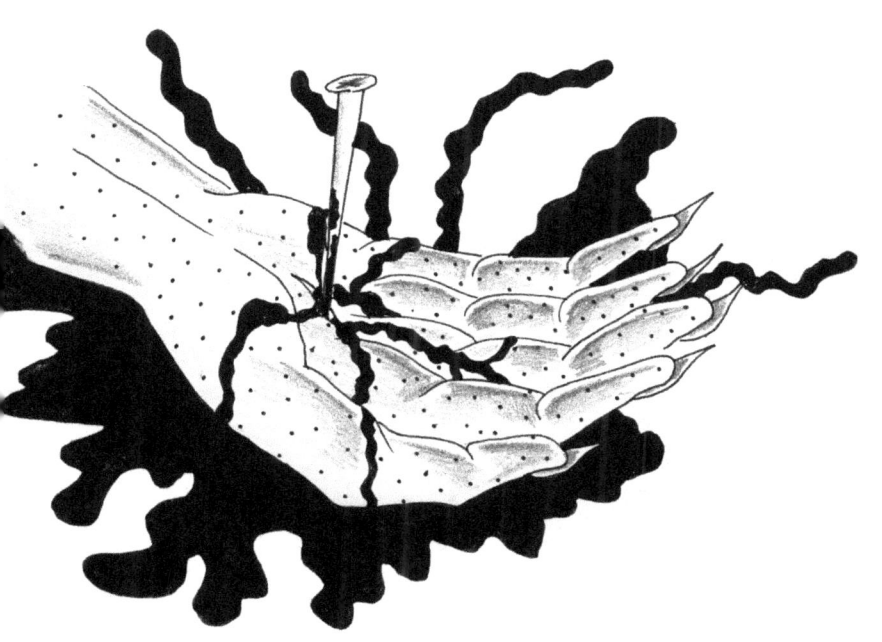

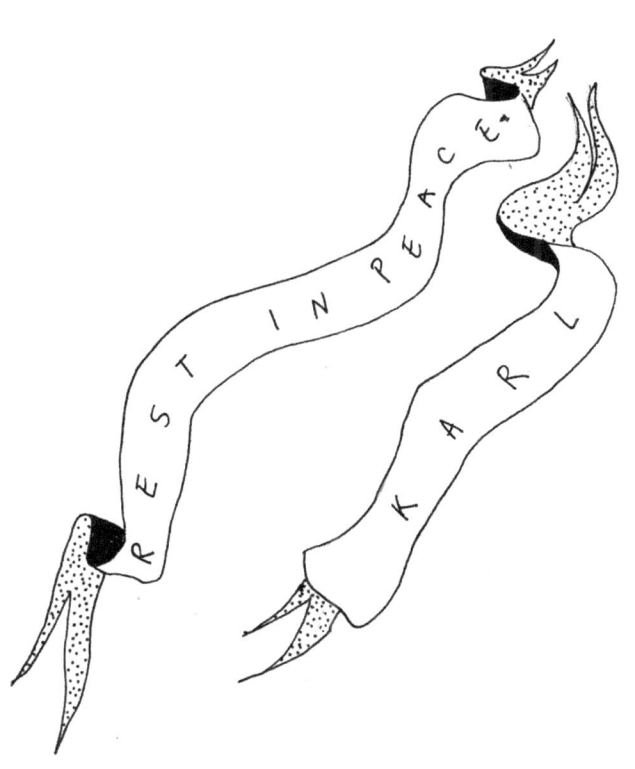

Jason Baldinger is a poet from Pittsburgh, Pennsylvania. A former Writer in Residence at Osage Arts Community, he is co-founder and co-director of The Bridge Series. He has multiple books available including *The Better Angels of our Nature* (Kung Fu Treachery) and *Everyone's Alone Tonight* with James Benger (Kung Fu Treachery Press) as well as the chapbook *Blind Into Leaving* (Analog Submission Press). His work has been published widely in print journals and online. You can listen to him read his work on Bandcamp and on lps by the bands Theremonster, and The Gotobeds.

Nell Hendricks is a multimedia artist born and living in Pittsburgh, PA. She works primarily in a knit medium, making 3-dimensional conceptual sculptures dealing with the subjects of trauma, grief, and mental illness. After attending Tyler School of Art studying printmaking for a few semesters, she dropped out following her dad's passing to pursue her own work. This is her first published work.

www.ingramcontent.com/pod-product-compliance
Lightning Source LLC
Chambersburg PA
CBHW050326120526
44592CB00014B/2074